When SAINTS GO MARCHING IN

HOW SOUTHERN BAPTISTS RESPONDED TO KATRINA

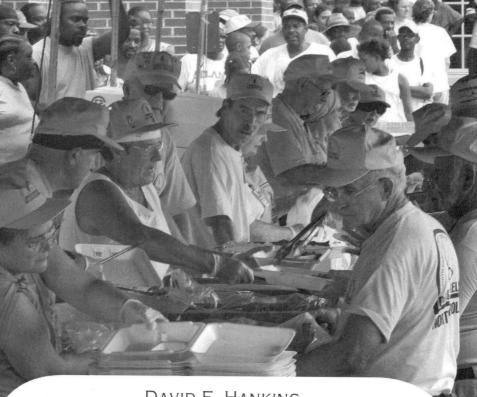

DAVID E. HANKINS
with NORM MILLER

NASHVILLE, TENNESSEE

PREFACE

"For the training of the saints in the work of ministry, to build up the body of Christ." (Ephesians 4:12)

The title of this book has a decidedly New Orleans flavor. The song "When the Saints Go Marching In" is a theme song of the Big Easy, associated with the city's French Quarter, its jazz musicians, and even its football team. The spiritual content of the lyrics rarely registers amid images of Mardi Gras parades, jazz festivals, and an all-around good time. Now, added to New Orleans lore and mystique will be Katrina, the dreaded storm that finally came.

Although Katrina hammered thousands of others in Mississippi and Louisiana, the destruction of one of the most famous cities in the country is the lead story. Everyone will remember the levees, the flood, those stranded at the Superdome, and an entire population evacuated, many never to return. Everyone will remember where Katrina hit: New Orleans. The story is one of help and hope for New Orleans and the Gulf Coast region.

The title also names Southern Baptists. We want to tell a little of our response in this large disaster. Are the Southern Baptists the saints? Not if you think a saint is some embodiment of perfection, or someone who is so high on the ascent of moral and spiritual achievement that mere mortals are put to shame. But *saint* is the designation the New Testament gives for those who, by faith, are followers of Jesus, and who (by his grace, not their own merits) are set apart as his servants; therefore, *yes,* we are saints! I certainly do not want to be self-congratulatory. I do, however, want to share a brief account of a remarkable ministry performed by my family of faith, the Southern Baptists. And this account is primarily for Southern Baptists, although everyone is welcome to read along.

I am indebted to Norm Miller, who accepted the assignment to help with this project. He has researched, traveled, photographed, collated, advised, and written. His contribution is substantial. Norm is a regular contributor to Baptist Press. Many others shared stories with us for which we are grateful. I am also indebted to my colleagues in Southern Baptist leadership who suggested I write this initial reflection on the disaster relief ministry, and to the SBC Executive Committee for sponsoring its publication and distribution. I hope that my proximity to the situation both geographically and chronologically has not caused my perspective to be skewed. I certainly understand all the facts are not in yet and much more remains to be discovered and written. As this book goes to press, Southern Baptist Disaster Relief has been deployed to south Florida in the wake of hurricane Wilma, an increasingly familiar necessity in that state. It seems apparent in these crucial days that Southern Baptists ought to be especially cognizant of the unique characteristics, the unique structure, and the unique opportunities God has given to us as a denomination. May the telling of these stories give us that awareness, and may we give glory to God.

CHAPTER 1

SOMETIMES THROUGH THE FLOOD

The western coast of Africa is like a wild baseball pitcher, hurling orbs of fury on a course of limited predictability. Those rotating balls of red and orange look menacing on the radar as they storm across blue ocean water. First a thunderhead on to a tropical depression, then a tropical storm with a name, next the gale hits fever pitch as a hurricane bearing torrential rains and knife-like winds that can cut a pine tree in half and not uproot it.

ABANDONED HOUSE
Photo by Jeff Woodrich

Though many houses in the New Orleans area escaped Hurricane Katrina's winds, this one and many thousands of others bore the brunt of Katrina's rain after levees protecting the Crescent City failed.

Hurricane Katrina was different, however, only in that she didn't spin off the west coast of Africa. She popped up over the south-eastern Bahamas August 23 as Tropical Depression Twelve. The next day, a hurricane, she hit Florida. Temporarily weakening over land, Katrina headed west-northwest across the Gulf of Mexico, defying predictions that she'd turn north. By August 29 at 6:10 a.m., Hurricane Katrina made landfall near Buras-Triumph, Louisiana, with sustained Category 4 winds of 145 mph. As she churned up the eastern Louisiana coastline, most communities in Plaquemines and St. Bernard Parish, and Slidell in St. Tammany Parish, were severely damaged by the storm surge and strong winds. A few hours later, Katrina made landfall for a third time near the Louisiana-Mississippi border with 125 mph, Category 3 winds.

The storm surge along Katrina's immense northeastern quadrant was of record proportion, smashing the Gulf Coast, including Bayou La Batre, Alabama; and in Mississippi: Pascagoula, Waveland, Gulfport, Biloxi, Ocean Springs, Gautier, Long Beach, Pass Christian, and Bay St. Louis. Katrina cut a damaging diagonal swath across Mississippi, affecting almost the entire state.

HOW FIRM A FOUNDATION?
Photo by Norm Miller

The fluorescent orange paint on the side of this house in the quaint seaside hamlet of Pass Christian, Miss., indicates a search-and-rescue team from Ohio found no one alive or dead in the house.

After the storm passed through New Orleans, it headed north across Lake Pontchartrain to the piney woods of St. Tammany and Washington Parishes. Huge oaks were uprooted while the pines were clipped off like match sticks at 10 to 20 feet high. The day after the storm the area looked like a helicopter had turned upside down, with blades 70 miles wide, and had gone through the area.

Katrina dropped mega-tons of rain, swelling Louisiana's Lake Pontchartrain and eventually breaching the levees that protect New Orleans and thus flooding that city. Hurricane Katrina is the most destructive and costly natural disaster in the history of the United States and has created a humanitarian crisis similar to the Great Depression. The official death toll exceeds a thousand, and damage estimates soar to more than $200 billion. More than a million people were displaced, and about five million were left without electricity. Federal disaster declarations blanketed 90,000 square miles of the United States, an area almost as large as the United Kingdom. Recovery projects will last months and years, not weeks.

UP TO THE EAVES
Photo by Norm Miller

For weeks after Katrina passed through the Gulf Coast region, houses in New Orleans remained flooded. This aerial picture of a New Orleans neighborhood was taken a week after the catastrophe.

Joe McKeever, director of missions for the Baptist Association of Greater New Orleans, spent September 29, 2005, checking on the city. It was one of the worst days of his life. He drove down deserted streets with destruction on both sides. McKeever saw an occasional worker cutting trees or stringing electrical lines, and a homeowner or two working in their yards, but not much more activity. Eerie was the silence in a city once populated by hundreds of thousands of people.

The floodwaters had drawn a cruel line in some neighborhoods, marking the height of their destruction on every house, business, church, and vehicle. The distinction between dirt and vegetation was gone. Every building, every car, every plant was the same gray-ish-brown lifeless color. Abandoned homes lined each street with the watermark touching the gables. Rarely, some churches appeared to be in good shape. But others were inundated with ugly toxic water that washed in and stayed for days.

McKeever was asked two months after Katrina hit, "Is the city getting back to normal yet?" He wrote, "You know, I wonder if they said that to the Hiroshima survivors in the fall of 1945. Because we

STAINED SANCTUARY
Photo by Keith Manuel

Gentilly Baptist Church, like so many other parts of New Orleans, provides silent but graphic testimony of Hurricane Katrina's sorrowful legacy.

won't ever be back to what New Orleans was before Katrina, and we're a long way from finding out what the new city will be."

To compound the destruction of Katrina, less than a month later, another hurricane, a Category 3 named Rita, slammed into the Gulf Coast at the Texas-Louisiana border. In preparation for this storm, hundreds of thousands of citizens from Lafayette, Louisiana, to Houston, Texas, fled to safety. Although not as traumatic as New Orleans, the evacuation of Houston was marked by stalled traffic, gasoline shortages, and at least one tragedy: a bus filled with elderly evacuees caught fire on the highway, killing several of the passengers. Communities in the storm path itself experienced widespread flooding, uprooted and broken trees, and destroyed buildings. Power outages and fuel and water shortages lasted for weeks in places like Beaumont, Texas, and Lake Charles, Louisiana. The impact was felt throughout east Texas and southwest Louisiana. This double disaster paralyzed the whole Gulf Coast from Alabama to east Texas. Louisiana was pummeled from border to border.

Everything was devastated, including the churches. Those of us who have responsibility to the churches began immediately trying to contact pastors and other ministers in the damage zones. Perhaps no other church gained more national prominence than First Baptist, Gulfport. Located just a few hundred yards from the shore, it took the brunt of Katrina's storm surge with catastrophic results.

Two churches Joe McKeever saw on his initial search tore at his heart the worst. One church had mud several inches deep in the sanctuary—windows blown out; the stench, unbearable. McKeever lifted his head to see the waterline several inches above the front door. Salt water had killed the grass and shrubbery outside, turning them brown. Silt covered the tops of cars parked on the boulevard's elevated median in front of the church.

McKeever saw the beloved and bedraggled New Orleans Baptist Theological Seminary, locked down and guarded by a company of police. All of the faculty houses—40 of them—were flooded and about 45 percent of the student housing was flooded.

Approximately 675 churches in Alabama, Mississippi, Louisiana, and Texas were significantly damaged by Katrina and Rita. My former congregation in Lake Charles had the east and west gables of their new sanctuary blown out, allowing the rain and wind to ruin everything inside. More troubling than the damage to church facilities, though, is the damage to church congregations. Will the members be able to save their homes? Will they have jobs when they return? Will they return at all? Some pastors in the New Orleans area estimate at least 50 percent of their congregations will not return. Some may lose even more. This could be true all along the coastal regions. What will be the future of these ministries?

WHY?

What ought we to make of this unprecedented natural disaster on U.S. soil? Considering the numerous hurricanes that had already smashed Florida in the previous fifteen months, many have begun to wonder if this is to be the new norm for this region. The economic, infrastructure, and lifestyle impact has reached unparalleled proportions. While other places in the world have suffered far more deadly and destructive upheavals (such as the Christmas tsunami and the recent Pakistan earthquake), these hurricanes' wrath can justifiably be described as "disaster."

Theologians, pundits, and the man on the street began immediately to ask (and attempt to answer) the question, "Why is this happening?" Environmentalists blamed global warming. Apocalyptics blamed sin. Government officials pointed fingers at each other for everything from inadequate levees and lack of preparation to failure to respond quickly and effectively. The bewildered, helpless, and grieving victims are wondering, too.

It is tempting, when tragedies come, to try to explain "why bad things happen." The question is in the larger arena of the problem of evil and suffering. One reporter called me and asked the question this way: "Did God cause Katrina to punish the people of the Gulf Coast?" The short answer to the question is *no*. While we affirm that all people are sinners and subject to both temporal and eternal judgment by God, we deny that the people of the Gulf Coast are any more in need of judgment than the rest of us (cf. Luke 13:1–5). Also, while we affirm that God will one day judge the living and the dead, we deny that every natural evil (hardship, trial, difficulty) is necessarily a punitive action of God. We testify of a loving God who is merciful, longsuffering, and forgiving.

When Christians have discussions on evil and suffering, several things are important to remember:

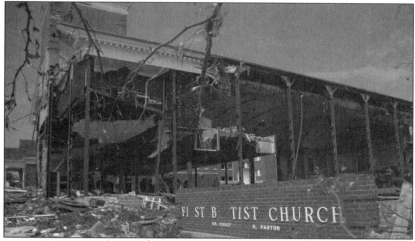

A GUEST UNINVITED
Photo by Norm Miller

Hurricane Katrina's storm surge at Gulfport, Miss., was reported at 28 feet. It proved too much for the 30-foot walls of First Baptist Church here.

1. We will not be able to take away all pain and mystery by our explanations. We are not God and must not presume to know everything God knows.

2. We must be guided by a thoughtful study of the counsel the Bible gives us. There is nothing wrong with listening to various thinkers on this thorny problem, but our authority for understanding the ways of God with men is the Bible.

3. Knowing that blessings may ensue from a tragedy doesn't mean we do not experience real sorrow and hurt. We should not gloss over other people's heartbreak.

4. It is not necessary to know the exact source of or reason for hardships that come our way to affirm that God is in control and can use every trial to develop our character and bless us and the world (cf. James 1:1–12).

5. Since we live in a world that is full of pain, we should learn to be grateful that God turns those things into vehicles for blessings. What are some of the blessings that could come from the hurricane devastation? Maybe these: recognizing how great it is to serve others; reordering priorities to put people before possessions and eternal treasures before temporal concerns; formation of new relationships; lessons on

prevention of future hardships; reminder of the brevity of life; the motivation to begin a relationship with God.

HOW?

I have tried to remind folks that, although it is important to discuss the nature of evil and suffering, it is not necessary to hold this discussion on the front end of the tragedy. Our first duty is to concentrate on helping. In the case of the hurricane victims, feeding, housing, giving, presence, and praying were more needful than philosophy.

This small book is an attempt to tell the story of a group of people who did just that—people who saw a great need and waded in chest deep to help. These people are called Southern Baptists. These hurricanes hit on their own turf. Eighty percent of the 16 million Southern Baptist members live in the southeastern United States. But even those who live outside the area rushed to help. This is the nature of Southern Baptists. We are particularly suited to crises response. That's the point I want to make in this book.

Don't misunderstand. Southern Baptists were not the only responders—not by far. People of various faiths and no faith from all over pitched in to help. Business and industry, government, charitable organizations like Red Cross and Salvation Army, and other individuals and groups gave time, money, and aid. We could not have met the need, nor did we want to, by ourselves.

But we are part of the story, and no one acted more quickly or more effectively than Southern Baptists. No one was better trained or equipped. Southern Baptists were the first in. They recruited massive numbers of volunteers and gave what was needed. And they are still on the job.

How were we able to do, by God's grace, what we have done? It is a result of our people, our convictions, and our organization. It could be outlined as caring people, congregational participation, and the Cooperative Program. Or as one Baptist leader styled it, Cooperative Hearts, Cooperative Churches, Cooperative Program.

The individual Baptist has a personal relationship with Jesus that gives him purpose, calling, and compassion. We are activists more so than theoreticians. We are constrained by the love of Christ to minister in his name. Ministry belongs to the people, not to some clerical hierarchy. This "every member a minister" belief makes us ready and willing volunteers. And that serves us well in times of crises.

Then, we believe in the local church. We are so committed to the concept that we have congregations everywhere—every village, every town, every corner. And these churches are autonomous. They have all the authority necessary to do whatever their hands find to do. There is no checking with "headquarters" to see if it is OK. They are empowered and organized to address whatever challenges may come. This book is, in large measure, the story of churches doing what their Lord has asked them to do.

Finally, Southern Baptists cooperate. The separate congregations have voluntarily formed associations and conventions in order to accomplish wide-ranging ministries. The longstanding, cooperative organizational structures and cooperative funding of Southern Baptists provided the mechanism, the experience, the planning, and the resources to tackle the demands of the hurricane disaster.

As we chronicle our response to Katrina, I pray we may celebrate what God is doing and be reminded of the unique and effective ministry we have together as Southern Baptists.

SEMINARY AFLOAT

An unidentified professor at New Orleans Baptist Theological Seminary took this picture as he was evacuated by boat from the seminary's flooded campus.

CHAPTER TWO

SBC DISASTER RELIEF

It had the efficiency of a military operation: central planning and coordination, strategic deployment of troops, efficient execution of duty, rapid mobility, and ability to engage on multiple fronts. This was not the Marines. It was the forces of Southern Baptist Disaster Relief, some 30,000 people who comprise the United States' third-largest disaster relief agency. And they were at the ready for Katrina. Having tracked the hurricane for days, SBC Disaster Relief coordinators and volunteers were mobilizing. Unlike the so-called friends of Job—who himself lost everything in a series of disasters—Southern Baptists didn't sit around offering every sort of verbal accusation and explanation, wringing their hands in the paralysis of analysis. Instead, being lithe and light on its feet, the SBC Disaster Relief organization swung into action—first on the scenes of devastation even before US government relief agencies and other charitable organizations.

"As soon as landfall is imminent, we go into action," said Jim Burton, coordinator for volunteer mobilization of the North American Mission Board (NAMB). "We've worked for 35 years to build capacity to respond to something like this. And we celebrate the ability to meet these kinds of challenges."

The first Southern Baptist Disaster Relief response can be traced to 1967 when a small group of Texas volunteers helped victims of Hurricane Beulah by serving hot food cooked on camp stoves. To this day, the SBC continues disaster relief ministries in aid to victims of natural and man-made disasters such as floods, earthquakes, hurricanes, tornadoes, fires, and terrorist attacks in North America and overseas—all in an ultimate effort to spread the gospel of Jesus Christ.

In 2004, Southern Baptist volunteers responded to 193 named disasters, prepared 3.5 million meals, repaired 2,683 homes, and removed debris from 10,704 yards. All assistance is provided to individuals and communities free of charge. The efforts of 2005 will prove to be significantly greater because of Hurricanes Katrina and Rita.

More than half of all mobile Southern Baptist Disaster Relief units have been involved in Katrina/Rita response, said Jim Burton. On the Thursday and Friday before Katrina came ashore, the entire SBC Disaster Relief network was on alert. "By Sunday (Aug. 28) we were making assignments and moving units. On Monday of land-fall, mobile kitchens, shower units, cleanup-and-recovery units and communication equipment from more than twenty states were staged near Memphis, Tennessee, and Marshall, Texas," Burton said. "On Tuesday, more than two dozen disaster relief units were on their way to devastated areas. And by Wednesday we were feeding

ENCOURAGING THE ENCOURAGERS
Photo by Norm Miller

SBC President Bobby Welch visited Katrina and Rita devastated areas many times. Here he encourages workers at an SBC Disaster Relief feeding unit parked at FBC Biloxi, Miss.

hungry people and getting ready to clean up their homes and remove downed trees from their houses and out of their driveways."

After Katrina flooded New Orleans, NAMB's 350-seat auditorium was made a disaster relief command center, complete with eight large screens, projectors and 42 workstations. A similar set-up was created at the offices of the Louisiana Baptist Convention in Alexandria, where staff and volunteers manned computers and toll-free telephone lines to coordinate needs with resources, and to keep communications lines open between NAMB, Red Cross, the state conventions, churches, and the front line ministries. A ham radio unit was housed at the Louisiana Baptist Building to communicate with disaster relief units while telephone service and e-mail were out of commission in the affected areas.

The American Red Cross had asked Southern Baptists to prepare 300,000 meals a day and be ready to increase capacity to half a million meals a day by the end of the week. During a natural disaster, the American Red Cross and the Salvation Army depend on NAMB to coordinate the 600-plus disaster relief units owned by SBC churches, associations and state conventions and staffed by

HEADQUARTERS FOR DISASTER RELIEF
Photo courtesy of NAMB

Staff members at the Southern Baptist Disaster Relief operations center are closely monitoring Hurricane Wilma as the storm approaches Florida's southwest coast. The center at the North American Mission Board in Alpharetta, Ga., has been an unusually busy place as record hurricanes have passed through the States.

Southern Baptist volunteers. These mobile units include feeding, chainsaw, mud-out, command, communication, child care, shower, laundry, and water purification facilities.

I visited one shower unit deployed to Covington, Louisiana, that had actually been constructed during the first few days of the Katrina response. It was so new, the yellow-and-blue disaster relief logos had not yet been applied. But it was providing showers for the first wave of chainsaw crews in the area.

"Southern Baptist Disaster Relief ministries continue to exceed all previous expectations," Jim Burton said. "There is no way that we can fully know today the extent of ministry that has taken place.

PARTNERS IN RELIEF

Photo by Norm Miller

According to the North American Mission Board, that SBC agency has prepared and served more than 80 percent of all meals at disaster relief sites sponsored by the Red Cross.

Beyond people being fed physically and spiritually, I believe that God will bless the faithfulness of Southern Baptists in this response to further grow this ministry."

The Disaster Relief Teams give eternal as well temporal aid. At FBC Pascagoula, Miss., George Swaringen was standing at the end of an SBC Disaster Relief food line, saying: "Who needs Jesus? If you're lost and need Jesus, come over here. You've got bread and water from the food line. But I'm passing out the Bread and Water of life." Swaringen, a layman from Antioch Baptist Church in Woodbury, Ga., helped lead several people to faith in Jesus Christ.

D. Waylon Bailey, pastor of FBC Covington, La., wondered whether anyone knew the extent of the devastation on the day after Katrina. Communication with the outside world was nonexistent. He was all alone. Then, he says, "The cavalry arrived." It was the

WHAT DO YOU NEED?
Photo by Norm Miller

Susanne Howard, member of Cottage Hill Baptist Church, Mobile, Ala., is flooded with requests for food, ice, baby items, and more from Katrina victims whose scores of cars were lined up on the street adjacent to FBC, Pascagoula, Miss., where Southern Baptists were manning a disaster relief station.

disaster relief team from his own state convention in Louisiana. For the next few weeks, he and his wife Martha joined the volunteers as they ministered to hundreds of hurting people who came to the church campus for help. They, too, saw spiritual victories. Bailey reported that a chainsaw crew working near where he lives led eight people to faith in Jesus Christ.

"You got diapers?" "Do you have any ice?" "I need some food." That's what Susanne Howard heard from victims as they spoke from their cars concerning the necessities of life. On a side street next to the church, cars were lined up for several blocks with the line extending several more blocks down an adjoining street. Despite a sweltering sun and the muggy Mississippi climate, Howard stood on the hot pavement, brushed sweat from her eyes and completed a checklist of supplies as motorists expressed their needs.

HOW DO YOU SPELL RELIEF?

Photo by Norm Miller

Tons of food, clothing, and household supplies crowded the parking lot of First Baptist Church, Slidell, La., where just a few days before people were catching stranded fish. About 5 feet of flood water invaded the church's first floor.

"Just give this list to the people on the lot, and they'll fill your order," she'd say with a smile and a "God bless you." Howard then directed the needy people toward the church parking lot, which looked like a truck stop. In each trailer were tons of disaster relief provisions.

Howard, from Cottage Hill Baptist Church in Mobile, Ala., said she volunteered for disaster relief because "my Lord, Jesus Christ, commands me to get out and help people when I can. My family's fine. My house is fine, and I have the resources to do so."

Inside the church, Jim Wood, 68, of Millry Baptist Church, echoed Howard's comments. "I had a little damage at my place in Alabama," he said. "My barn roof is laying out in my backyard—so what?"

"I'm healthy, and I just love to help people. I've done that all my life. When I find someone who needs something, I want to help all I can, and I try to let them know the help is coming from the Lord," he said.

Nine students from the Baptist Collegiate Ministries at the Alexandria campus of LSU traveled to southeastern Louisiana for disaster relief ministry. Along with sorting clothes, serving about 1,600 hot meals, and distributing ice, water, and MREs at the SBC Disaster Relief site at FBC Slidell, the group joined a chain saw crew headed to Mandeville.

Intent on cleaning trees and debris at the house of the Nobles, a young couple from the Life Church in Mandeville, the team first removed a huge tree from their unchurched neighbors' backyard at the Nobles' request.

Gretchen Nobles later e-mailed the team: "You guys have no idea how much of a blessing it was to have your help. . . . Please know that your impact has been much more than just cleaning trees and leaves. We had just moved to this neighborhood, and you have really helped me have an open door to share Christ with my neighbors."

Pastor of FBC Pascagoula, Rex Yancey, said, "On behalf of my church, I'd like to thank Southern Baptists for what they're doing. What the people here need now are not words, but actions. And when the local people see the words 'Southern Baptist' written on these [disaster relief] trucks, and see the people wearing yellow shirts in these serving lines, they know there's hope."

LINING UP

Photo by Sherri Brown

A serving line opens for Hurricane Katrina victims in Pascagoula, Miss., manned by Georgia Baptist disaster relief volunteers.

Folks in hurricane-isolated Bogalusa were just as thrilled to see the yellow shirts. Bogalusa, Louisiana, became cut off from the rest of the world. Trees made roads impassable, and most electrical and telephone lines were down.

Bob Adams, pastor of FBC Bogalusa, La., along with others, had hunkered down at the church. They were running out of supplies and water and were unaware that anyone knew about the plight of the community.

The situation became desperate, and hope was fading. Then the sequestered victims saw people in yellow SBC Disaster shirts cutting through the debris, followed by a feeding unit. Adams and others said the SBC's disaster relief efforts there lifted the spirits of the whole city.

Scottie Stice, director of missions for the Del Rio-Uvalde Baptist Association in southwest Texas, had this take on SBC Disaster Relief. Stice and his disaster relief chainsaw crew were out to aid Hurricane Katrina victims, but Hurricane Rita had other ideas: "We were at our rally point in San Antonio when our deployment was changed. We had local church members composing our disaster relief teams from our own association and two others, the Frio River and Hill Country associations. Our guys were on the phone with the guys at the Southern Baptists of Texas Convention, and they were talking to people at the North American Mission Board. And then it struck me: This is one huge cooperative effort—local churches working through the local associations, and associations working through the state convention, and the state convention working with the national entity. I thought it was a perfect illustration of how the Cooperative Program should work," Stice said.

Stice's story doesn't end there. He explained in an October 13 Baptist Press story how the SBC's Cooperative Program and Disaster Relief led Clyde Lummus of Kirbyville, Texas, to faith in Jesus Christ.

Clyde and Rose Lummus huddled in their small house as Hurricane Rita stormed up the tree-whiskered hill country of east Texas. The only noises louder than the howling gale were the monstrous oak tree crashing through their roof and the stately pine tree crushing a pickup truck in their front yard.

Stice and his chainsaw crew spent a day and a half removing the wooden intruders. Clyde stayed inside almost the entire time

FIRST THINGS FIRST
Photo by Norm Miller

Scottie Stice, director of missions for the Del Rio-Uvalde Baptist Association in southwest Texas, spends a few minutes reading Scripture and praying with his chain saw crew before tackling the day's work.

NOT A COMPLETE LOSS

Photo by Norm Miller

Hurricane Rita's winds destroyed two-thirds of the house owned by Clyde and Rose Lummus of Kirbyville, Texas. The portion of the house that was spared was the original cottage-like structure of their home. The truck in their front yard didn't fare as well.

and, to Stice, Clyde seemed to be "an old cowboy, self-made, self-sufficient." But when the chainsaw crew finished the job, Clyde tearfully thanked them.

A few days later Clyde was crying again. He had just responded to an invitation to pray for repentance from his sins and commitment of his life to Christ offered by SBC President Bobby Welch, who was touring east Texas and had stopped to preach in Kirbyville.

Stice saw Clyde weeping. "I put my hand on his shoulder and asked, 'Did you pray to receive Christ?'" Stice recalled. "And he said, 'I sure did.'"

Stice describes disaster relief work as "a tool the Lord can use to reach people for evangelism. In the midst of suffering we have a chance to minister the gospel and a ray of hope with someone by giving them a hot meal or by mudding out their house or by getting a tree off their roof."

Stice said Southern Baptists are blessed to have the Cooperative Program "because it led to meaningful ministry, and it led Clyde Lummus to Jesus Christ."

Take a look at the statistics for Southern Baptist Disaster Relief to Katrina and Rita through October 25, 2005:

State Conventions Activated   41
Volunteer Days Contributed   116,637
Meals Prepared   9,369,355
Jobs Completed (cleanup and recovery operations)   13,661
Showers Provided   67,095
Laundry Loads Completed   15,532
Children Cared For   7,526
Messages Sent   3,056
Gallons of Water Purified   9,295

If Southern Baptists had waited until Katrina hit to decide how to help, it would have been too late. The thoughtful, prayerful planning and working across the years by denominational staffers and volunteers all over the nation has created a world-class disaster ministry, as indicated by the testimonies and the statistics above. Without the SBC's Cooperative Program, this kind of expansive and expedient ministry wouldn't happen. While almost all financial support for disasters comes from special gifts in response to crises like Katrina, the Disaster Relief organization is made possible by the Cooperative Program. NAMB earmarks some of its Cooperative Program funds for disaster relief training resources and travel. State conventions generally have staff members like Sam Porter from Oklahoma and Loy Seal in Louisiana who organize and train the many volunteers at the local level. These staff leaders are supported by the Cooperative Program. "The Cooperative Program is the empowerment to do disaster relief on the scale we are able, and it provides the infrastructure that makes disaster relief possible," Jim Burton asserts. "Unlike other charitable relief agencies, we can expend one hundred percent of disaster relief monetary gifts for that specific purpose because of the Cooperative Program."

Some Baptists may have wondered if their regular Cooperative Program gifts make a difference in peoples' lives. Southern Baptist Disaster Relief answers with a resounding yes.

CHAPTER THREE

HOUSES OF HOPE

"The hurricane disaster is propelling the church to be the church." This is the sentiment I've heard from pastor after pastor in the last several weeks. One of the truly noteworthy results of the Katrina tragedy is that, when the ordinary emergency procedures of government and relief organizations were overwhelmed, the churches stepped in to meet the needs and have stayed with the process to completion. Churches gave money and provided volunteers for the Disaster Relief organization. The most useful spontaneous response, however, was the ministry to evacuees. Hundreds of thousands of people were driven from their homes. Unlike many other storms, this one did not permit a quick return. The designated shelters were beyond capacity immediately.

Southern Baptists stepped up. Within five days of Katrina's strike, NAMB announced an initiative it called Houses of Hope. President Bob Reccord said, "We are asking for churches with facilities that can be converted into temporary housing for evacuees to become Houses of Hope. Our encouragement would be to begin with an initial commitment to house evacuees for 30 days, with a subsequent review for an extension." NAMB staff began a process to register churches, coordinate responses, and assist with pertinent how-to information. "Our greatest opportunity and privilege is this: In the process of giving not only hope for today and tomorrow, hope for eternity can be shared with those to whom every church has the opportunity to minister," Reccord said. "And that is the reason for which we as Christ-followers exist!"

This was one denominational emphasis that required no coaxing of the churches. In fact, scores of churches around the country had already offered their facilities for such use stretching from

Houston to Memphis and Nashville. Other congregations banded together at Baptist campgrounds to take care of evacuees. One of our strengths as Southern Baptists is our congregational autonomy. Not one of our churches needed to call me or anyone else to get permission to serve. They simply attacked the need. With or without an official name or sign up, these churches became Houses of Hope. It was amazing to watch.

FBC Jackson, Miss., opened its family life center as a shelter, but later transformed it when officials at the health and human services center of Jackson called and asked if First would be willing to house elderly and infirm people who were evacuated from nursing homes along the Gulf Coast.

"The nation is watching to see if those of us in the Bible Belt will turn our backs on these people," said First member Jean Young referring to all hurricane victims. "God expects us to step up to the plate, and this is the time to do it."

FBC member Rebecca James, the district health officer for the Mississippi Department of Health, said, "If you just let Southern Baptists know you need help, they'll pile in and do it."

SHELTER AND CARE
Photo by Norm Miller

Medical Student Richard Bush examines Nancy Whitehead of Slidell, La., at a shelter for evacuees at FBC Jackson, Miss.

Lee Thigpen, director of the shelter at First, estimated the shelter had aided as many as 200 people in its first four days of operation. Choking back the tears, he said many of them attended the Sunday morning worship service at the church. "At the end of the service, many of them came down front. All they wanted was a hug."

A few miles up the road, Broadmoor Baptist Church's Christian Life Center, located in suburban Jackson, was abuzz with the shrieks of children playing, adults jabbering, and televisions blaring. But Ann Southerland maintained a calm demeanor and broad smile when the telephone rang, interrupting her conversation with a family checking into the center.

"Do you have any clothing or basic foodstuffs?" one woman asked Southerland, peppering her with even more questions in rapid-fire succession. "We don't know how long we're going to be here. Do you have any commodities we could have? We left Metarie [La.] without anything. What about food staples like rice or potatoes or canned goods we could have? Me and my husband are on Social Security and our checks were mailed to our home, but we have no way of getting there now. My husband's over in Lafayette [La.] with our older daughter," the woman related, hardly taking a breath.

Southerland smiled as she dropped toothpaste, shampoo and other personal care items into a plastic bag for the woman.

In the adjacent gym, where cots and inflatable mattresses dot the floor, new sheets billow as Al Jernigan and Becky Greenleaf prepare the beds for new arrivals. Both are members of Colonial Heights Baptist Church in Jackson.

"Any way Christians can minister—I think that's what we're called to do," said Greenleaf. "We're called to stop doing what we think is important and to take care of the other more pressing needs for these people."

In my own state of Louisiana, I was both humbled and overwhelmed at the response of our churches. I traveled all over this state in recent weeks, and I have yet to find one of our churches that did not do something significant in disaster relief.

Some of them like FBC, Houma and Istrouma, Baton Rouge, both within an hour of New Orleans, were official Red Cross shelters. Houma sheltered both evacuees and Red Cross volunteers. It became a full-time job for Pastor Steve Folmar. He organized volunteers, reallocated space, coordinated distribution of resources

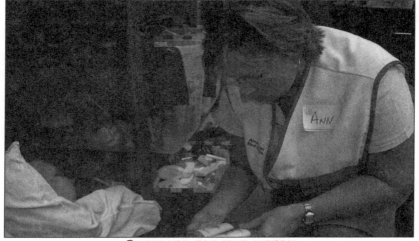

SUPPLIES FOR THE NEEDY
Photo by Norm Miller

Ann Southerland sorts through donations during her 6 p.m.-to-midnight shift at a shelter for Hurricane Katrina evacuees at the Jackson-area Broadmoor Baptist Church in Jackson, Miss.

like food, water, and clothing, and negotiated "jurisdictional issues" among the various helping agencies. Most importantly, the church met the physical and spiritual needs of the victims.

Istrouma organized its entire church life around the evacuees' needs. Pastor Stuart Rothberg said, "Our church program is now two Sunday morning worship services and this relief effort." As I walked through the campus with the pastor, I was amazed at the level of organization and ministry, performed mostly by volunteers. Half of the campus was the shelter for the several hundred evacuees. Church members had constructed large men's and women's shower facilities and a laundromat adjacent to the church buildings. Services such as filing government forms, security, education, job placement, and haircuts were arranged. The evacuees were organized with duties for caring for themselves and the facilities. And the largely African-American evacuees were becoming, through worship and ministry, part of the largely Anglo congregation.

The other half of the facility was a supply center for evacuees throughout the region. Church volunteers sorted and arranged all kinds of clothing, toiletries, and other items. Evacuees waited in a lounge area with refreshments while a "personal shopper" recorded their needs and then retrieved the items for them. The system was a demonstration of efficiency and compassion.

Other churches simply volunteered their facilities without an official designation. Pastor Paul Roney encountered a caravan of evacuees along the road in Alexandria, three and one-half hours from New Orleans. When he discovered they had no place to stay, he had them follow him to the church. He called church members, and they began preparing and bringing food. This small congregation was now a House of Hope.

Churches in the far northwest part of the state also helped. FBC Bossier City is one of those churches. Pastor Fred Lowery said of evacuees from the Gulf Coast, "They came to us by the thousands, literally, and our church members became the first responders. [Evacuees] were getting off of buses cold, wet and afraid, but there was nobody to help them except the church of Jesus Christ."

First Baptist provided food, clothing, cots, bedding, and even turned its chapel into a distribution center. Meeting those needs brought opportunities for even more ministry. "City officials were calling asking for help, saying, 'You're the only ones I know who can get this done or meet that need,'" Lowery said.

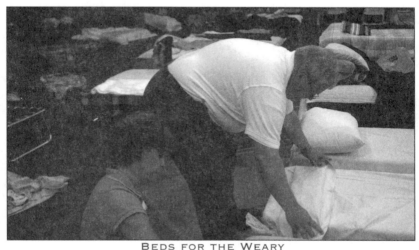

BEDS FOR THE WEARY
Photo by Norm Miller

Becky Greenleaf and Al Jernigan help prepare beds at the Jackson, Miss.,-area Broadmoor Baptist Church's shelter for Hurricane Katrina evacuees.

ABOVE THE GROUND

Photo by Norm Miller

Aboard a rescue helicopter, SBC President Bobby Welch (right) surveys prop-
erty damage to churches in the New Orleans area. Accompanying Welch are
David Hankins, Pastor Fred Luter of New Orleans' Franklin Avenue Baptist
Church, and Pastor John Faull of Williams Boulevard Church.

The local fire department conducted a fund drive and gave the
proceeds to First Baptist because, they said, "You're the ones on the
front line," Lowery recalled.

Members at Judson Baptist Church in Walker, La., rallied in disaster relief, transforming their facilities into a shelter for displaced
people, as well as a collection-and-distribution center for disaster
relief supplies the church received every day.

The 18-wheeler loads of supplies were miracles in themselves,
said Judson member Jeff Woodrich, who explained that many times
calls asking for very specific items would come to the church from
many miles away, and just that day the church had unloaded a
truck with those very supplies.

A week after Katrina hit, some members of Judson who are part
of the Louisiana Baptist Builders and who were constructing the
Global Maritime Ministries building in New Orleans wanted to
assess damage to that building.

Judson member Ed Jelks contacted Port Chaplain Philip Vandercook. He contacted the harbor police to get permission, which was granted conditionally. The police required those who assessed the damage to bring Bibles and to minister to the harbor police force.

"Isn't God awesome? Not only did he allow us back into the city, but he provided an opportunity to witness for him," said Jelks.

The team from Judson trekked into New Orleans, carrying almost three tons of food, clothes, and other supplies. "Every checkpoint opened with no problems or questions," recalled Jelks. "When we got there, the harbor police were overwhelmed."

The assessment revealed about $15,000 in damage to the Global Maritime Ministries building, but Jelks and others kept making deliveries and ministering to the harbor police, the US Army Corps of Engineers, the Army National Guard, and another Guard unit at New Orleans Baptist Theological Seminary. At the National Guard facility, Jelks and others organized a praise and worship service in the security office.

On one such delivery, Woodrich had to block traffic to unload his trailer-full of supplies as there was no good place to get off the road. Woodrich had a sign on the vehicle that read "Acts 1:8 in Action!" In just a few minutes, a policeman in full SWAT gear was tapping on the truck's locked door, alarming Woodrich at first.

"Sir, I understand what Acts 1:8 means, and I want to thank y'all for praying for us," the policeman told Woodrich. "But I have one personal request right now. Would you get out of your truck and pray with me?" Woodrich prayed with the man right there.

Woodrich got back in the truck and prayed again: "Lord, if I had only sat at home and watched this on TV, I would have missed being a part of your work."

The list could go on and on. FBC Gonzales is fifty miles west of New Orleans. The church became the relief coordination center for the whole parish, helping evacuees obtain, among other things, appropriate prescription medicines. Churches like Florida Boulevard in Baton Rouge and Summergrove in Shreveport became warehouses for the receipt of donated goods and the distribution of those goods to the evacuees. FBC Baton Rouge used its facilities for an important ministry niche. They housed and cared for mothers with newborns. Tommy Middleton at Woodlawn Baptist, Baton

Rouge reported 30 professions of faith among the evacuees they cared for. Could this be the beginning of our churches' finest hour?

Several observations come to mind from this tremendous hope-giving ministry by the churches:

- Congregational autonomy is not only biblical, it is productive. How I rejoice at the constructive, compassionate, and evangelistic care of the churches for the evacuees. Unleash the church!
- Having congregations everywhere is a great plan. Every church—large and small, white and black, country and city—had a strategic opportunity. Let's plant more churches!
- Churches get more kingdom work done when they open up to the community around them. Let's not wait for a disaster to become Houses of Hope.

Some Christian organizations have been suggesting their strategy is superior to denominationalism because they deal pastor-to-pastor and congregation to congregation. No red tape. I applaud their emphasis on the local church. But they didn't invent it. Southern Baptists have been practicing that for a long time.

A SIGN OF HOPE
Photo by Jeff Woodrich

The sign on the side of the truck driven by Jeff Woodrich—associate mission church builder of the Louisiana Baptist Convention—caused a policemen to stop and ask for prayer.

CHAPTER FOUR

ADOPT-A-CHURCH

Southern Baptists had some particular concerns in the aftermath of Katrina. As they ministered to the thousands of citizens who had fled the path of the storm, the news of unprecedented damage made its way to the public. Damage estimates evolved into more accurate assessments, and the reality was not pretty. There had been massive—in some communities, virtually total—destruction of businesses, homes, and economies. The particular concern of Baptists was for their church buildings, ministers, and congregations. These were savaged by the storms like every other facet of the community. Southern Baptists, as has already been noted, wasted no time in coming to the aid of the hurting populace. Now, with the same sense of urgency, they moved to help their broken churches. Multiplied hundreds of churches suffered damage ranging from roofs blown off to the entire facility washed away. In New Orleans and other low-lying regions of the Gulf Coast, many church members lost everything—their homes and their jobs. The implications of this for congregational life are still being assessed.

"All these churches are just devastated," said disaster relief volunteer Ken Whitton, who is student pastor at Dayspring Baptist Church in Mobile, Ala. "Kind of a big thing is we preacher boys live off of tithes, and when your community is not working, there are going to be a lot of pastors who are going to be at the mercy [of someone's kindness] just as anybody else is. What do you do?"

Something had to be done—and in a hurry. Within a week of Katrina's landfall, the SBC accomplished something not too short of miraculous for any organization, especially one of its size. The SBC's North American Mission Board rolled out a compassionate and comprehensive initiative.

Along with the Houses of Hope initiative previously mentioned, Bob Reccord and the North American Mission Board announced the initiative called Adopt-a-Church. Reccord said Adopt-a-Church would pair "healthy and blessed SBC congregations across North America" with other SBC congregations whose facilities were badly damaged or destroyed. "This will be a commitment of anywhere between one to two years. All manner of help will be needed: mission trips, rebuilding trips, care packages, appropriate financial support, and encouragement for the staff that have been through numerous challenges."

Reccord intimated that several smaller churches could band together in aid to just one church in the Gulf Coast region, saying that no church is too small to participate and that it would take multiple partnerships to assist each church.

The need for churches to join the Adopt-a-Church effort could be no more poignantly illustrated than by this account from what happened to a church in Mississippi. The pastor fled the hurricane and later returned to find his home and church completely destroyed. While the pastor was on his way to Jackson—where the Mississippi Baptist Convention offices are located, and where he would seek

STORM SURGE

Photo by Norm Miller

Pews at First Baptist Church in Pass Christian, Miss., looked like toppled dominoes after they swirled in the surge of Hurricane Katrina.

help and consolation—he received a call telling him not to come back to the church because the members had decided to join other churches that had weathered the storm.

Another pastor from a small congregation south of New Orleans that had only ten families was told by seven of the families that they may not be returning to the area. This kind of news came to small and large congregations alike—a significant proportion of their pre-Katrina congregations would be unable or unwilling to return to the area. It is not difficult to imagine the impact of this on the future of the churches. Will they be able to keep the staff? Can the bills be paid? What will the ministry look like?

In early September, 20 pastors and church staff in the Baptist Association of Greater New Orleans met in Jackson, Miss., for encouragement and information. On Sept. 28, the group met again with 40 present at FBC LaPlace, just west of New Orleans.

Before Hurricane Katrina hit, the New Orleans association had 75 churches and 60 missions. But those numbers are no longer valid, and it is not certain just how many churches—or church members—will remain as people begin returning to the city. Gulf Coast pastors and staff members spread out across the United States, and now many are returning to their fields of ministry. Many, however, are still lonely and feeling low.

Helping to lift their spirits in the September 28 meeting were Louisiana Baptist Convention personnel, who distributed financial aid to each pastor and staff member. The funds are from the convention to specifically help affected church personnel. The initial grant to affected ministers in Louisiana totaled over $1.1 million. Additional supplements will go monthly to those in need. LBC staff also gave the pastors information packets detailing how to participate in NAMB's Adopt-a-Church program.

The goal of the Adopt-a-Church program is to help hurricane-stricken churches to rebuild their facilities, encourage pastors such as those noted above, and repopulate their flocks. My challenge to Southern Baptists is to take care of every pastor and staff member for at least one year who was on the job when the hurricane came. Some will find congregations in other places. Some will be able to be sustained by their current flock. Many will need to be adopted by other congregations. This may take the form of salary supplements or providing health care premiums, or adding the staff member to the staff of the adopting church for some period of time. The state conventions, with the help of Southern Baptist contributions, will underwrite much of this salary supplement process.

"This is a great way to go. We want each church to have about a dozen or so sponsors. They're going to need more help than any one church can do," DOM Joe said.

Like Houses of Hope, the Adopt-a-Church concept resonated with Southern Baptists. Calls began to come in, volunteering to adopt, even before assessments of those in need could be completed. In Louisiana, every available program staff person was reassigned to act as a coordinator or advocate in the Adopt-a-Church program. Assisted by local directors of mission (DOMs) and some staff from NAMB and the Florida Baptist Convention, each of these coordinators took 8–10 hurricane damaged congregations to help with assessments and arrange for help from adopting churches.

As of October 31, 160 congregations in Louisiana had applied for adoption. They have been partnered with 652 congregations across the SBC. In Mississippi, 222 churches have been adopted by 1,129 congregations. The commitments made by adopting churches vary. Some will give a love offering. Others have provided a salary for a staff member. Others are planning mission trips for cleaning, rebuilding, or evangelizing. The strategy is to partner enough congregations with appropriate resources with the churches in need plus supplements from Southern Baptist general relief gifts so that each congregation is made whole for the near future.

Another strategic goal of the Adopt-a-Church process, is the long-term re-congregationalizing of the devastated areas, such as New Orleans. This will take careful study and prayer, and plenty of resources over the next few years. The pastors and other leaders in the New Orleans area do not know what shape the city will take as it rebuilds. David Crosby, pastor of First Baptist Church and Keith Manuel, pastor of Calvary Baptist Church, have heavy hearts for their city. In a recent planning meeting to discuss ways the two churches can respond to the need, Crosby expressed his heart: "Hurricane Katrina has devastated our city. More than 50,000 homes in Orleans Parish sat in salt water for weeks. Help is needed for individuals to rebuild their homes and lives."

With strong emotion Crosby continued, "Whoever steps in with assistance in this very personal and strategic endeavor will secure a

voice in the city's future . . . evangelistic opportunities will abound."
Thus was born the Orleans Parish Recovery Plan.

The Orleans Parish Recovery Plan is a cooperative effort of the
two New Orleans churches, the Louisiana Convention, NAMB, and
other Baptist entities to help Orleans Parish residents rebuild their
homes and lives. The recovery process includes mud-out and clean-
out, replacing dry wall, and then restoring electrical power.

Initial funding for the Orleans Parish Recovery Plan is coming
from Southern Baptists' gifts to the Katrina Relief Fund. This will
allow the local churches to be strong enough to take the lead in
reaching out to their city. Volunteers from around Louisiana and the
nation are needed to do a variety of jobs. But the most important
job is giving hope in the name of Jesus. That's the heart of two New
Orleans pastors and thousands of Southern Baptists.

Plans like this will be formulated wherever needed within the
damage zone. We are committed to being prepared and active so
as to accomplish all God wants in evangelizing the "new" Gulf
Coast and New Orleans. Bringing the local churches to full strength
is the key to long-term ministry and outreach. Adopt-a-Church is
making that happen.

CHAPTER FIVE

ADVANCING TOGETHER IN RANKS

The Bible often gives us lessons for life from nature. Proverbs 30:27 says, "Locusts have no king; yet they advance together in ranks" (NIV). The ancient world knew the destructive power of locusts. These small creatures were unimpressive individually. No one of them was a superhero who could take charge and lead them to success. But en masse they were a formidable force. They could destroy the vegetation of an entire region. They could fill up all the houses in several villages. They could blot out the sun. Locusts, says the Bible writer, know the power of cooperation.

Baptists, like the locusts, have no king. We do not have prince or pope or council to tell us what we must do. But we have understood the power of cooperation. And we have harnessed it. Recognizing that no single individual or church can accomplish all God wants done in missions, Southern Baptists banded together to reach the world. We have advanced together in ranks.

THE NETWORK WORKS

I have never been prouder of our denominational family than I have been during the post-Katrina recovery. As a citizen of Louisiana and one who has responsibilities for statewide Baptist ministry, I am grateful for what Southern Baptists have done for us. I know my counterparts in other affected states share my sense of gratitude. Hurricanes Katrina and Rita have given an opportunity for all to see why the historical structures of Southern Baptist life are so valuable. I have already summarized what Southern Baptists churches did and are doing through the Disaster Relief system and

Houses of Hope and Adopt-a-Church. But that's not all the story. The official organizations of Baptists at every level were immediately engaged in response to this crisis.

I am particularly proud of our SBC president Bobby Welch. He has demonstrated since his election in 2004 that he did not intend to be only a figurehead. That was no more clearly manifested than in his involvement in disaster response. Dr. Welch quickly arranged travel to the damaged regions, visiting Mississippi, Louisiana, Alabama, and Texas, and then came again. He surveyed the damage, encouraged the pastors and other leaders, brought supplies and gifts, prayed with the relief volunteers, and witnessed to victims. The president arranged meetings of state convention and SBC leaders, talked with government leaders and the media, and challenged all Southern Baptists to rally with aid for our needs.

Other SBC leaders like Morris Chapman and Bob Reccord and their associates were on the scene, offering comfort and counsel, as well as Louisiana Baptist Convention president Philip Robertson. My counterparts in other state conventions acted quickly to help us. Some of the first assistance came from the Florida Baptist Convention. They had experienced four hurricanes the previous season and had learned many lessons and seen amazing response. John Sullivan and his staff and churches provided immediate relief, great advice, and an unusually empathetic response. They had been there! I got calls, e-mails, and letters from Baptist denominational leaders from across the United States.

The help wasn't merely talk. The Southern Baptist network provided the resources we needed to minister to the victims of the storms, especially our pastors and churches. The SBC Executive Committee voted to send all Cooperative Program receipts over the budget for disaster relief, and to send more as needed. That made available approximately $12 million for New Orleans Seminary, NAMB, and the three state conventions. These dollars would have gone to all the SBC entities, so each of them had a part in this generous gift. The two mission boards allocated millions more from their reserves or disaster funds for the needs of the hurting and damaged churches. LifeWay trustees set aside $6 million for disaster relief and sent funds immediately. Guidestone Financial Resources waived three months' medical insurance premiums for their constituents in the affected areas, and offered other relief. All six seminaries offered adjustments in funding ratios so that New Orleans Seminary would have extra help from the Cooperative Program during the recovery from the calamity.

The state conventions also gave generously. Numerous state conventions collected gifts from their churches and authorized expenditures from reserves for those of us who had been ravaged by Katrina. Gifts are still coming in. Already the contributions from the state conventions total several million dollars. In Louisiana, we received numerous gifts from individuals, churches, associations, and some charitable organizations that have been very helpful. Almost 90 percent of the disaster contributions, however, came through our ministry partners at the SBC and state convention level.

We believe our Baptist family will be with us until all needs are met. As is always true in Southern Baptist life, all the gifts go directly to the relief work. We are not deducting money for staff or regular budgeted needs. We have already dispersed several million dollars to aid displaced pastors, meet expenses of the churches, and begin the repair process. This would not have been possible without Southern Baptist help. And Southern Baptists would not have been as able to help were it not for the Cooperative Program. The generous giving of the churches through the Cooperative Program made possible most of the disaster relief funds we have received.

We have also been helped by the loan of staff members from NAMB, Florida Baptist Convention, LifeWay, and Oklahoma Baptist Convention. These wonderful folks, along with many volunteers, assisted our staff at a critical time in our response. Other state staffers came with disaster relief teams from their conventions.

Another part of the network that needs to be mentioned is the Baptist association. The DOMs from the affected areas were on the job at once, searching for displaced pastors, visiting church sites, assessing damage, and helping in disaster relief work. Several of them had personal losses since they live and work in the storm area. In spite of that, they became contact points for their churches, conduits for support coming from the state convention and elsewhere, and organizers of disaster relief operations.

The state convention staffs also played an important role. Disaster relief became our only agenda and everyone was on the disaster response team. John Sullivan said this has become standard operating procedure for Florida Baptist employees during hurricanes. Jim Futral in Mississippi deployed his staff to the disaster task as well. I am so proud of our Louisiana state convention staff. From Baptist collegiate directors to Sunday School strategists to administrative assistants, everyone joined the effort and was glad to do it. By noon, the day following the flood of New Orleans, when we knew this was no garden-variety disaster, our employees had set up a command center with banks of computers and telephones, had created software applications to manage the overwhelming data that would come in the next several weeks, and reassigned the duties, some to man the center and the rest to be out in the field. We didn't stop for six weeks. We are still working on it at a steady pace. It is our new work.

This network—disaster relief, communications, financial backing, staff organization, coordination with local churches—didn't have to be created after the storm hit. It already existed. It is how we get God's work done. Not only did it make a disaster response possible and effective, but also it allowed our other ministries to continue. Except in the damaged areas, Baptists kept on with their extensive national and worldwide work. The collegiate ministries got underway this fall as usual. Thousands of seminarians are in class. Not one of our 5,000 missionaries had to return from overseas because of Katrina. Evangelism training, family advocacy, and church planting continues apace. No single church working alone could make that happen. It takes all of us. The network works. That is the power of cooperation.

THE ROLE OF THE COOPERATIVE PROGRAM

The lynchpin of this intricate and expansive Baptist network is the Cooperative Program, the Southern Baptist missions funding process. Some of us have been engaged in a lengthy and intensive dialogue about the future of the Cooperative Program, and the current Katrina crisis provides an excellent opportunity to include *you* in the dialogue.

A little history may be in order. In 1845, Southern Baptists had created their new Convention for the purpose of "organizing a plan for eliciting, combining, and directing the energies of the whole denomination in one sacred effort, for the propagation of the Gospel." Their early efforts were valiant and fruitful, but they were hampered by lack of resources. The number of denominational enterprises and institutions was growing. Each needed support. Each ministry affiliated with the SBC and the many state conventions raised its support independently of the other ministries. Each went about seeking the contributions of the congregations. Sunday by Sunday, fundraisers from seminaries and colleges, orphanages and hospitals, mission boards and benevolent organizations fanned out among the churches asking the faithful for help. Some fared better than others. Some years were better than others. The gifts were distributed unevenly. The more popular, or perhaps the swifter, received a disproportionate share of the offerings. Other important ministries went begging. It was feast and famine.

Furthermore, the costs of raising the money were sometimes as high as 50 percent of the proceeds. The churches were beleaguered by an endless stream of denominational representatives needing "pulpit time" to make their appeals. On the whole, the results were discouraging. No one was being adequately supported. Too much energy was being expended in the process by both the ministries and the churches. The growth of stewardship in the denomination was not keeping pace with the growth of obligation and opportunity. The Cooperative Program was initiated in 1925 to replace all the independent and competitive practices. Churches could now give one set percentage of their income to support all the ministries. Now there was a common mechanism that would allow every Baptist enterprise to have the support it needed. The results have been nothing short of miraculous.

From the early 1930s until the mid-1980s, gifts to the Cooperative Program grew from $2.4 to $330 million. On average, churches were giving almost 11 percent of their undesignated receipts to the Cooperative Program. Such widespread, aggressive support made it the premier missions funding method among denominations.

But in the last several years, there has been erosion in Cooperative Program support by the churches. For example, for decades, the regular increase in a church's Cooperative Program percentage was promoted as a virtue, and was a sign of a healthy Southern Baptist congregation. Since 1984, however, there has been a marked change in support for the Cooperative Program from the churches. While total dollars have continued to grow, reaching $500 million in 2003, and while the percentage of churches giving through the CP remained at a remarkably high 95 percent, the percentage of the churches' undesignated receipts began a serious decline in 1985, falling from 10.6 percent to 6.6 percent in 2005—a startling 33 percent reduction.

There are some reasons for this. Chad Brand and I have addressed this subject more fully in our book *One Sacred Effort* being released by Broadman & Holman on May 1, 2006. Briefly, the erosion generally coincides with the erosion of biblical stewardship among many Baptist church members. Some people who may give a love offering in a time of crisis like a hurricane neglect the regular gift of a tithe through their local church. Statistical evaluations show a serious decline in tithing the last thirty years.

Furthermore, there appears to be a growing tension between local church direct missions and local church cooperative missions. This is a great concern. Southern Baptist strength, as the Katrina response has shown, rests on twin pillars: (1) the autonomous local congregation and (2) the cooperative denominational network. Both are essential. Neither should be neglected or underemphasized.

Many churches are doing both direct missions and admirably supporting the Cooperative Program. The number of local church short-term mission projects has risen dramatically over the last three decades. These volunteer ventures have made a tremendous contribution to kingdom work. They find support and coordination through our conventions. I have participated in numerous overseas mission trips. They are a good thing.

But a caution is in order. Congregations must be careful to use direct mission involvement as a supplement to cooperative missions, not as a substitute for cooperative missions. My concern is for those who choose direct missions instead of Cooperative Program support. The dark side of direct congregational mission ventures is the temptation to withdraw support for the whole range of worldwide ministry carried out through the conventions. While a congregation may find great fulfillment and a degree of fruitfulness in direct missions, if the larger common work is neglected, have we helped the kingdom of God to prosper?

What if what was intended as an unleashing of the local church ends up as undirected hyperactivity that lacks focus and longevity? Could we mistakenly substitute enthusiasm, romance, and adventurism for constructive, effective, efficient, and lasting kingdom advance? We all remember the hapless Forrest Gump who, in a fit of enthusiasm, jumped from his moving shrimp boat to swim to shore to greet his friend, leaving the boat to crash into the piers. Are we jumping ship from one of the greatest vehicles God has given in order to pursue impulsive short-term, isolated endeavors? Will our proven kingdom enterprises be wrecked on the shoals of non-cooperation?

I am disturbed when some suggest the denominational missions approach tells churches to "pray, pay, and stay out of the way." They imply convention mission strategy is cumbersome, unresponsive, and unable to harness the power of the churches. This is certainly not true of Southern Baptist denominational missions. Have the facts been examined? Are new methods better, or are they simply a return to the failed independent societal approach to missions from decades past? The Southern Baptist mission model, undergirded by the Cooperative Program, is an extremely effective and efficient process for evangelizing the world. Independent, untested methods ought not to be substituted without careful examination.

Congregational entrepreneurial missions are not mutually exclusive from cooperative missions. They work perfectly together. Each congregation must pray through its own response. Southern Baptists leaders are currently challenging churches to adopt an Acts 1:8 strategy that involves each congregation in mission commitment in its "Jerusalem, Judea, Samaria, and to the ends of the earth." The goal, as articulated by John Sullivan of Florida, is to have a plan that evangelizes "everywhere, all the time, at the same time." Nothing accomplishes that like the Cooperative Program. Disaster Relief in the aftermath of Katrina is a great example of Southern Baptist-created, Cooperative Program-supported, local church-executed cooperative missions. The point is, however, we do this all the time—24/7—in a hundred different ways all over the world.

Perhaps a great blessing to come from Katrina will be that Southern Baptists who have been tempted to pursue other mission strategies will be reminded of the great value of advancing together in ranks through the Cooperative Program.

THE CROSS IN THE CRISIS

New Orleans Seminary student Mike Whitlow and his wife Kasey hardly had time to get anything before the onrush of flood waters at the Gentilly Apartments. Weeks later they were back, trying to salvage anything they could. Pretty much everything was lost, its value smothered in muck.

Ed Jelks of Norwood Baptist Church helped the couple, but all they retrieved was Mike's military graduation ring and a coin collection of about $400. Kasey was almost frantic about a 6-inch crystal cross. It was a gift from her mother that Kasey had used on her wedding cake. She was looking forward to passing the cross to her own daughter one day. The couple thought the cross might be under the refrigerator, but they were unable to move it. They left. Kasey was crying.

Jelks went back a few days later to look for the cross. He called his wife to tell her the search was in vain. "Don't hang up the phone," she said. "You keep looking, and I'll keep praying."

Blindly fumbling, he felt it. "Had my hand not been guided, I would never have retrieved the cross," Jelks said.

When Jelks gave the cross to Kasey, he said, "Even when every-thing seems to be destroyed, we can know that nothing is ever lost at the foot of the cross."

How important it is for this to be said! So many people found out that things they hoped would support them couldn't hold up in the hurricane. The levees couldn't hold up. Their houses couldn't hold up. In some instances, the government couldn't hold up. Their jobs couldn't hold up. But there is One who can hold up. Jesus holds up through any storm—wind, water, illness, betrayal, poverty, sin, or death. Nothing is too great for him.

Retired pastor Donald Denton's testimony captures the essence of this truth:

You may have seen a picture on CNN, in *World Magazine,* or in some other publication of a sign that was erected in front of a home where a pile of trash of the personal contents of that family had been thrown out. I was there that day . . . . I had no idea it would receive such notoriety, but we were there helping to mud out . . . repair . . . and clean out that home. The son of the couple had stayed with us since the time the home was flooded. He found a piece of plywood that had been used to cover some windows. He found a can of gold spray paint and he said, "I'm gonna make a sign and put it out front." He painted on it—"OUR LIFE IS NOT IN THIS PILE OF STUFF BECAUSE OUR LIFE IS HID IN CHRIST." When he got down to the word *Christ* and painted the *C* the paint ran out. He went back and he found another can of gold paint, and he got out the letter *h* when the paint ran out again. He said, "Satan is trying to stop this, and I will not be defeated." He went back and almost miraculously found a third can of spray paint (this one was white), and he finished the word *Christ,* and it stood out. Soon a man came up to Lee's wife, who was sitting in the yard, and said to her, "I want to give you something," and he gave her a hundred dollars. She said, "I can't take that." He said, "Please take it. I was so despondent . . . in such despair, . . . and the message there restored my faith."

In the midst of despair and the muck of disaster, where so much was lost, the cross of Jesus Christ was not lost. In the hearts of his followers, it began its triumphal march into the Gulf Coast, days before devastation. When the flood waters receded, the cross was raised in New Orleans, a red one on a Christian flag. And the love of Christ is still waving over the entire Gulf Coast as Southern

Baptists march together under that blessed banner, doing unto others as Christ would have them do.

The goal of Southern Baptist Disaster Relief is not just to give temporal help but also to give eternal help. Sam Porter, who leads Disaster Relief for Oklahoma Baptists, reminded us at the outset of the Katrina disaster, "They could probably get someone else to set up feeding units. Baptists do it because we want to share Jesus."

Along with food, water, and chainsaws, Southern Baptists have taken Bibles, gospel tracts, and personal testimonies into the disaster zones. Many have already received Christ. Many people are attending churches in their neighborhoods for the first time because Baptists were there when they needed help.

SBC President Bobby Welch reminded us that each act of help and kindness should be performed in Jesus' name. Will there ever be a time when hearts are more tender or when eternal matters are more on people's minds? Welch challenged, "Both those who need help and those who offer help are especially sensitive. Share Jesus with everyone."

COMPASSION UNFURLED

Paul Blange, recently resigned pastor from Metarie, La., wanted the Christian flag he duct-taped to a street pole a few blocks from the Superdome to remind all who saw it of Southern Baptists' concern for those displaced by Hurricane Katrina. David Hankins and New Orleans pastor Fred Luter assisted Blange.

Pray for many more to come to Christ. Those of us who have been concerned about resistance to the gospel, especially in New Orleans, are praying the winds of Katrina will be followed by a fresh breeze of the Spirit of God. Before God is done with this, may there be thousands of new "saints" along the Gulf Coast.

"But as for me, I will never boast about anything except the cross of our Lord Jesus Christ." (Galatians 6:14)